'Baby-tism of fire'
Our Journey to forever: an adoption story

To my fellow big who has held my hand during the hardest times and lifted me up when I have needed it.   You have made me laugh until I have nearly peed and been my sanity in moments of madness. Thank you for being my girdle. I love your face.

And finally, to our teeny wee human. I hope that you always know that your daddy and I loved you before we knew you and will love you when we fade and become stars. You are brave, beautiful and remember to aim for the stars because if you fall short, you will achieve the earth!

'May your choices reflect your hopes, not your fears.'

There are many reasons as to why people become adopters, and I would argue that no two adopters have the same story even though some of them may sound similar. For us, our journey to adoption is not unique, but the further along the path we venture we learn that it is unusual. We chose to adopt because we wanted to have a family, but adoption was never our last hope at having one, it was our first. We always wanted to have a family through adoption rather than through biology.

Now, our social workers have told us how unusual this is, but we don't really understand why.

*

The journey and experiences mentioned within these pages are ours. We are sharing them because we feel that adoption shouldn't be the last option for people to become a family, it should be a choice explored in the same way that IVF, IUI, surrogacy and giving up is.

Chapter and verse

1. Every journey starts with a step
   How we arrived at adoption as the way to start our family

2. The Stages
   The stages you go through to become approved adopters

3. Transition
   Meeting your teeny wee human for the first time and getting ready to become a family

And so the Babytism begins…

4. Never wake a sleeping baby! Never
5. And so the visits begin; one social worker to another
6. Living with uncertainty
7. *'Close encounters of the third kind'* Contact
8. Meet the parents
9. One small step for us… one giant leap to forever: placement order
10. …And it's a match: matching panel
11. Living in limbo
12. Applying to court
13. Disorgansied chaos: waiting for dates
14. The judgement
15. There is always one more hurdle to get through: waiting for appeal
16. Celebration
17. And that's a wrap

Chapter 1
Every journey starts with step…

My husband and I always talked about adoption as being the way in which our family would eventually be formed. I never had the desire to be pregnant and I do not believe that being a parent is defined by biology, and my husband wanted to be a parent but didn't really care how it happened; and as someone who is adopted himself he was 100% accepting of my desire to adopt.

After being together for 5 years, we got married, and after a few months we started to explore the idea of adoption and whether it was something we could pursue. We were living in Hampshire at the time, so we picked up the phone and called the Local Authority's adoption services. We asked questions and were asked questions in return, and we were told that we wouldn't be eligible to adopt as my husband was working away on wind turbines at the time and therefore we would not be suitable candidates at the time. Disappointed, but pragmatic we saw it as a sign that it was not the time. We continued with living as a couple; travelling, working and enjoying each other's company. A few years past, we moved overseas for a couple of years, gaining more life experience and memories as a pair. We moved back to the UK, this time to Bedfordshire, and we returned to our enquiries to adopt. We were ready. We had been together for 11 years, married for 6 years, had good jobs, owned a house (even though we were renting) and were financially secure. This was it, it was time. I called a local adoption charity, and two Local Authority adoption services to see whether we could start our journey to becoming a family. Again, we were told that we couldn't start the process because we hadn't been back in the UK for a year, once we had been back in the UK for a year we could start the process. We were dejected and disappointed, but we were resolute in our decision to adopt and we knew one day we would. Chances had it, our landlord had sold the house we were living in and we had to move again, which meant that we were house-hunting for our home. So maybe, just maybe, we weren't quite living at the right time to adopt.

A year past, we had bought our home, carried out a lot of renovation work, and we felt ready to be a family…again. We were nervous about enquiring about adoption again as we had had a series of 'no you are not suitable' responses. Now I am a great believer that all important decisions should be done by pulling a name out of a hat, by sticking a pin in a map or whilst in the bathroom (don't ask why – I think it is because it is hard to walk away from a conversation if you are in the bath or on the loo). One night, my husband and I were in the bath having a chat (as you do) and we discussed how we were going to become a family, we aren't getting any younger after all. As we had been knocked back in adoption we decided to give biology a whirl.

In theory, biology should be the easiest way to have a family. I mean people get 'accidentally' pregnant all the time, or they only did it 'once', they were drunk, or they didn't think it would happen to them. I may have been in my mid-30s but I was fit and healthy; surely it would be easy! WRONG!!!

We made the decision for me to come off the pill which I had been on for 16 years, and we were going to be grown-ups and make the active decision to try to create a human. Everything was going well; my husband thought every day was his birthday, my body was doing what it was biologically supposed to do…for a while. After a couple of months, I was late. Was this it? We bought a pregnancy test kit, and I did the glamourous thing and peed on it whilst probably peeing on my hand a bit – it is not a glamourous or ladylike experience. There was no smiley face on this one. For someone who is always punctual, I was just late. No baby. I was not knocked up. And this pattern repeated for a couple of months, until I wasn't late at all. My cycle had disappeared. When I hadn't been greeted by Aunt Flo for over 100 days we started to be faced with the reality that my body was not performing as it should do. We decided to go to the Dr and ask questions, to find out some answers. The Dr was concerned as I was 35 years old and time and Mother Nature can be a bit of a devious mistress when you get to your mid-30s. I was sent for blood tests and was told that I had PCOS – polycystic ovarian syndrome. I was given tablets to try to start a period, if that worked then we would have to wait to see if another one came. If it came, we would have to wait again. If it didn't we would be referred to a specialist earlier.

Even though biology was not our intended journey, we had started on the road and we had to see where it was going to end. We made the decision not to wait, but to seek advice from fertility experts. The fertility road is paved with vulnerability, heartache, being prodded and poked, but it is also filled with moments to laugh at. I have found throughout the whole journey, is that if you don't find humour in it, you will only find frustration and that will make you bitter – so laugh! And laugh out loud. I am a huge Victoria Wood and Julie Walters fan – two soups – and whilst sat in the fertility clinic waiting for my husband to return, I could imagine a Wood's and Walter's sketch being played out.

Would you like a cigarette dear? Maybe a smoking jacket?

Sitting in the waiting room, I couldn't help feeling tinged with anger and guilt. Anger at the fact that we were on this fertility path and it wasn't our desired method to becoming a family. And guilt because it didn't matter to me if I couldn't have a birth child, but also that I felt as though I was letting my husband down – even though I wasn't.

After two rounds of clomid and two rounds of injections, and my body not cooperating at all: it was like a defective typewriter, we were told that even with IVF we would have less than 10% chance of conceiving. We were not prepared gamble on biology any more.

We were now returning to our original plan: adoption. Even though we were pulled down the biology route because of knock backs in adoption, it was supposed to be our journey because it bought us back to where we were supposed to be. But now, we would never have any what ifs regarding biology.

Our adoption journey officially started in October 2016 when we went to an information evening at our Local Authority adoption services. We sat in a room with several other couples who were waiting to see if adoption was going to be a realistic option for them. We were told about what the process entailed, how long it would take, and how the children ended up needing to be adopted.

At the end of the meeting we filled out of expression of interest to pursue adoption and were asked about when our fertility treatment had ended: it had ended at the beginning of October, so we were told that we had to wait 6 months to deal with our grief at not being able to conceive. It didn't matter that we didn't feel that we had lost something not being able to have biological children, it was policy. Frustrating though it was having to wait even longer to start the adoption process, it was a finite period: we could start the adoption journey in April 2017.

Chapter 2
The stages

The adoption process is divided into two: stage one and stage two, and the government guideline is that the two stages should be completed in 6 months. In reality it is quite unusual for the two stages to actually take six months. It is quite common for prospective adopters to have a break for six months between stage one and stage two in order to complete certain things or to wait out this period due to a change in circumstances.

Stage One
In April 2017 after waiting six months to overcome our non-existent grief, we started stage one. During this stage you attend three sessions called *'Adoptive Parenting Training (APT)'* and during these sessions social workers and volunteer adoptive parents talk to you about adoption. We walked into social services child services centre and were greeted by 5 other couples all on the same journey from this day as us. The way we arrived at that point may have been different, and our paths may change and deviate from this point, but we were all on the same course as each other.
We found Stage One informative but frustrating at the same time. The focus was very much on the brain: reptilian and mammalian. That adopted children are quite primal and reactive in their behaviours because they would have experienced trauma regardless of the age they were adopted, due to the choices their birth parents would have made. They explained how the children who are needing to be adopted may have experienced multiple homes before they find their forever home. And the general intimation was that all adopted children would have some form of additional need…because they were adopted.

Now, as an educator of nearly 20 years I found their analogies to be somewhat damning in themselves and limiting. I felt that they were encouraging prospective parents to parent trauma into their child[ren] rather than parent them to understand and deal with the experiences that they may have had, especially if they are cognitively aware of them. My husband is adopted, and we have other family members and friends who have been adopted. All their journeys have been different, but they do not illustrate the messages that we were being given. We sat in one session when a social worker stated that 'all adopted children are damaged, traumatized and broken'. A statement that I have quoted time and time again to social workers and stated how damning that sentiment is in itself: limiting and damaging.

The reality is this. Most children who are waiting to find their forever, will have come from awful backgrounds. That is why they are being adopted. As adopters it is our role to be parents and to be unconditional in the love we have for our teeny wee human, and that we are, as adults and parents, supposed to help the teeny wee humans manage their feelings, emotions and experiences. The average age of a child being adopted in the UK is currently 4 years old. A 4-year-old will have some awareness and understanding of the world around them. They will identify with people and they will seek security and protection. A 4-year-old will not understand the world as an adult does, so it is important that they find themselves in a world where people will be their main stay, people wont budge no matter how hard they are pushed, and they will be loved and cared for unconditionally. They also need to be parented by people who can help them navigate their world of emotions no matter how big and overwhelming they may seem at times.

I've digressed. So, in Stage One you are told a lot about the experiences of the teeny wee humans waiting to be adopted and the impact that this may have on them. You look at some 'made up' profiles and are asked to choose which profile you would be drawn to as an individual. This was quite interesting as it illustrated whether you and your partner's ideas were aligned. You explored the roles of people within the adoption web to try and empathise with each party: the birth parents, birth siblings, adopters, adoptee, social workers. The adoption journey is not one you do in isolation, there are many parts to it and having an understanding and appreciation for the experience of each party allows you to go into the journey with eyes wide open, rather than eyes wide shut.

Remember that most children waiting to be adopted are not waiting because they have been relinquished. The majority are waiting because their birth parents have failed to offer them safety and security, whether that is through neglect or addiction.

In stage one there is also an optional session you can attend for Foster to Adopt or FFA. We found this session to be the most positive session, even though it is the session that fills adopters with more uncertainty and places them at greater risk.

What is FFA? In order for a child to be adopted, the social workers have to have looked and assessed the parents and the family network to see if there is anyone biologically linked who could parent the child. If, after their investigations, no one is found to be suitable, the court will make the child subject to a placement order. Once the placement order is in place then the child is eligible for adoption. In foster to adopt cases, the investigation into the parents and the family network is not 100% complete and therefore there is no placement order. There will be a care order in place and possibly a protection order which will be why the child is in care. Rather than the child being taken from their birth home, placed in foster care, possibly moved again in the care system, and then be placed for adoption, in FFA cases the prospective adopters become the foster carers and the first and only stop to adoption, reducing the moves and uncertainty the child will experience.

As an FFA carer you may be expected to facilitate contact with the birth family in a contact centre, you cannot call yourself mum and dad, you have to be cleared as foster carers as well as adopters, and you may be expected to keep records for the supervising social worker as foster carers.

During stage one you are also expected to complete homework – a book about you as a couple and as individuals. This contains your views on religion, education, diversity, family, as well as your chronology of key events every year since birth and your eco-map (who is in your network). Parts of this document will help to form the basis of your meetings and interviews in part two.

After we completed stage one, I changed jobs to somewhere closer to home, on more money and with less pressure but it was deemed by social services that changing jobs is stressful and therefore we needed to take a 6 month break between stage one and starting stage two. During this break we had to provide a detailed breakdown of how we could afford for one of us to be on adoption leave as my husband is self-employed: and being self-employed is deemed as being a financial risk to social service even if there has been no break in work and earning for in excess of 10 years.

As a result, we started stage two in January 2018.

As experiences go, we found stage two to be a continuation of the frustrations we felt in stage one, however stage two felt more of an intrusion like you are put under a spotlight. I remember our first meeting, we were told by the social workers that they weren't there to judge us, but that is exactly what they were doing. They were judging us and depending upon their recommendation we would be put in front of the elusive panel 4 months after the start.

During stage two you are met once a week pretty much for 4 months. We are asked questions about what we thought about various things: what our relationship was like, how we managed with pressure and stress, what our own up-bringing was like, what additional/ environmental needs would we be able to cope with when being matched to our child. We had to show our bank statements, the equity values of our houses, what assets we had, we had to have medicals going back to the first recording in our medical files. We were questioned, examined and assessed.

At the end of stage two, your social workers produce a document on you based on the two work books you produce over the two stages, this document is called the Prospective Adopters Report or PAR. It is this document that is shared with panel and the social workers of potential child matches.

Once you complete stage two you go to 'panel'. Panel seems like an elusive and mysterious thing that you hear about throughout your adoption journey, and you don't really comprehend what it is like, regardless of the preparation that your social workers do with you, until you walk into that room and are faced with boardroom tables and 8 people who will question and quiz you. Your future and possibility of becoming a family is held in the hands of 8 complete strangers, who have only read a report on you, and get to ask 8 questions.

We had our green-mile moment on Monday 23rd April, the day after we had run the London Marathon. Luckily, the DOMS hadn't set in by the time we walked into the room and we were able to sit down without wincing. We walked into the room and we asked a range of questions: fortunately, we weren't asked anything where my mouth would have caused debate – like 'what is your opinion of the adoption process?', 'How would you cope if the birth parents have additional needs or low IQ?'

After our questioning we were asked to leave the room whilst they discussed their recommendations. The chair person of the panel returned to our waiting room after a couple of minutes and asked us to return to the panel room. This time the green-mile felt like a couple of steps. We were nervous, obviously, who wouldn't be? Whether or not we were able to be parents rested on that moment and those people. We sat down and looked at the group and then we heard the words 'we unanimously agree that you should be allowed to adopt.' We were accepted. We were now officially dually approved adopters and now we were able to dream about the 'when' and not the 'if'.

The funny thing about being approved is that nothing changes, we still weren't parents, and unless the Virgin Mary's miracle of immaculate conception extended to those who were not in the 'biologically blessed' category, we certainly weren't pregnant. We were still waiting, and we still had no idea how long the waiting would last.

Once you enter the 'approved' list you are given access to a national database of children waiting to find their families. You are expected to scroll through lists of children and decide, based on two-dimensional information, whether you are their parents and they are your child. It is like being given a catelogue and asked to choose what you want. You are told the more time you spend looking the sooner you will find your family. For us, the more time you spend looking, the more upsetting and awful you find the experience. How do you choose?

We spent a couple of days looking and found it impossible.

The whole experience, whether looking through the data base, or attending 'profiling events' is as soul-less as buying a house. You look at the descriptions, if you like them, then you put in an expression of interest, and if the child's social worker likes you then you can proceed.

After three weeks of waiting, I received a phone call, and we experienced a monumental pee-on-stick moment. Our social worker, and for the purpose of personalisation and ease I shall call her 'Doris', called me up and said that the social worker (who I shall call 'Mavis') of a baby had requested our PAR (Prospective Adopter's Report aka everything except our blood group document) and was interested in us as a match for her charge. It was the end of the working day, and my birthday, so of course I went into meltdown and called my fellow Big like a mad woman possessed. Now, in the spirit of digression, we had spent a long time postulating (good word) about what we would do at this moment, and I had spoken to my gal-pal at work, and told her to expect me to become a blithering idiot, and I did not disappoint. You mentally prepare for this moment, but you can never really prepare for this moment.

I called my fellow Big and in his composed 'man' manner, he calmly went through the 'oh my gosh!', 'goodness', 'holy crapbags' response. When we got home that night, we discussed what Doris had said to me. We went through everything that we knew and we had to make a decision based on what we had been told. There was a Teeny Wee Human that has been born. It was a girl. She was known as 'Baby A'. She was in hospital still. Doris made it clear that there were uncertainties as the Teeny Wee Human would be placed under FFA and therefore we wouldn't know a lot of information. My Big and I were never put off by uncertainty because if you birth your own human then you get what you are given: you have uncertainty beyond biology – 50:50 DNA.

The following day we spoke to Doris and told her that we were interested in Baby A, and the following day she came round to discuss, to see if we had any questions, and to find out what our decision was.

I can't remember whether this took place over a day or three, but it was quick. We went from waiting, to possibly having a baby within days.

We were a 'yes'.

A week later we met with Baby A's 'family finding team' to see whether we were all in agreement that we were a match. It was during this meeting that we found out the name of our Teeny Wee Human and saw her picture for the first time. We had been chosen for her, and we are glad that we were. We didn't need to know her name or to have seen a picture to know that we were supposed to be a family, but seeing her picture and hearing her name (knowing it wasn't a car, country, drink or real name spelt wrong) only solidified our decision. We wanted to be Baby A's parents. Now it was all a case of 'when will it happen?'

We had mentally prepared ourselves for October/ November, not May or June – we were excited, crapping ourselves, and woefully unprepared: neither of us had every changed a nappy. And have you seen baby arms, they are terrifying – how do you get them into clothes without snapping them off? In our hedonistic moment of euphoria at the prospect of becoming parents, there was a lot of discussion about whether we would start transition immediately by going into the hospital to help care for our Teeny Wee Human, when I would be expected to go on adoption leave, what would we need to buy, etc. etc.

It is quite possible at this point that you are thinking 'what is the panic about, loads of time has passed...' to put this into context, we found out about Baby A on a Tuesday, the following Thursday we had met with the Family Finding Team and agreed that we wanted to proceed, the next day, Friday was my last day of work. Luckily, my employer has been amazingly supportive and they were only happy and excited for us, rather than monumentally pissed off that I was going on leave with 24 hours notice. A week later, the day before my fellow Big's birthday, we started our transition into becoming 'bigs' for the first time.

Chapter 3
Transition

They call the metamorphisis from non-parent approve adopters to parents 'transition', and this is because you go through the process of meeting your new bundle of joy, finding out information from your teeny wee human's foster carers... as well as buying lots of stuff, sorting your house out, managing your meltdown, and getting yourself organised as much as you can be.

Transition is exhausting. You spend 12 hours a day in the house of a complete stranger, getting to know your teeny wee human so that you are prepared to become Bigs to them when they eventually move home for the first time.

Our transition happened over a protracted period of time because our teeny wee human was going on her hols...well, her foster carers were, and because the system couldn't get itself organised quicker we couldn't start transition earlier so our teeny wee human could come home before going on her jolly jaunt to the Isle of Wight.

I remember the day we met our teeny wee human like it was yesterday. My fellow big had been at work, I went to the foster carers' house on my own and waited outside in my car whilst my fellow big hurtled his way to us – obviously keeping to the speed limit all the way! This was the first time that we met Mavis which in itself was quite nerve-wracking, what if she didn't like us? So there I was, stood near my car like a lemon, with our social worker Doris, being lead by Mavis to the foster carers' house, hoping that my fellow big would hurry up and get there, Mavis went into the house whilst we waited, and in the true sense of punctuality, my fellow big got there on time...just.

This was it! We were going to meet Baby A for the first time.

Now, I am what I would like to call socially stunted, if not inept. I don't do well with people that I don't know because I am shy and quite conscious that I am like marmite. My fellow big is someone who everyone likes, like nutella, but is quite happy to stay quiet which in moments such as this we needed to be our opposite. Fortunately, the teeny wee human's foster carers made things a lot easier for us because they are so warm and welcoming.

We crossed over the threshold of (for the purposes of illustration I shall call them Frank and Alice) the foster carers' house and were lead into the lounge with Mavis and Doris. We were greeted by a small red bassinette contraption and a tiny teeny wee human that was sleeping. Like rabbits in headlights and somewhat gormlessly, my fellow big and I just stood staring at this little bundle of life, giggled at each other and fell in love with our teeny wee human for the second time. We had no idea what protocol was, so our moments of being gormless felt as though they lasted for ages until Alice said; 'you can hold her, she is yours.' What an utterly bonkers idea. We went into that house as a two, and in principle at that moment, even though it wasn't for two more weeks and 6 more months, we were leaving it as a three. Mind-blown!

After Alice said we could hold her, we both looked at each other as if you say 'go one, you do it', we still stood there. I think Alice in all her awesomeness read the situation well, and scooped up the sleeping tot and placed her in Adam's arms – it was his birthday after all.

It is weird, in the most intensely emotional and overwhelming moment, as adopters you are 'watched' at how you respond to the teeny wee human and how you would react, but in a strange split universe surreal moment, you become absolutely oblivious to the social workers who are in the room with you.

We were only there on the first day for a couple of hours, enough time to have first cuddles, a cup of tea and to finalise the plan of transition.

The following day, we went to Frank and Alice's house for a few hours and experienced our firsts (we obviously resumed our established 'awww' position over the red bassinet to start the day). Our first scoop up the baby. Our first nappy change. Our first bottle feed. We were rocking the grown-up learning to be parents apron and we were embracing the challenge. I think Alice and Frank were a bit surprised that neither of us had changed, fed or clothed a teeny wee human before ... we are after all well established into our 30s (which is a polite way of saying closer to 40 than 20).

The end of day two was really strange, we knew that we weren't going to see the teeny wee human for 11 days, and even though we had only known her for two days we were going to miss her. We were truly smitten kittens.

We had started to prepare ourselves for the 'what if...'when we got approved as adopters so we had started to buy things, and nest (for some reason a feathery based metaphor is appropriate for getting your house together pre-welcoming a teeny wee human home: I don't know why?!). We knew that we would adopt a child who was under 4 years old, we always wanted a tiny teeny wee human (which is why FFA was our preferred pathway), but we wanted to be prepared for all eventualities. We had set up the nursery with a cotbed, suitable for a brand new human up to 4 years old and a changing table with storage.

We had ventured to Mothercare to make the sales assisitants feel uncomfortable asking for pram advice for a child you a) aren't pregnant with b) don't know when they will arrive and c) don't know how old they are... there is nothing more amusing than saying you are having a child when you are a size 10/12 with a flat stomach, and then watching their faces look confused and not sure as to whether they should ask 'when is it due?'

Buying a pram is like buying a car. Men look at the mechanics, maneuverability, and suspension, whereas women look at the aesthetics and whether or not it is a) heavy and b) have a large storage basket underneath for all your shopping needs. We went to Mothercare three times before we decided on the 'travel system' we wanted. After we had met Baby A, we were given the OK by Doris to by the baby carrier contraption thing too, as she was under 6 months and we would need one of those.

Eleven days to shop when you are utterly clueless is not a lot of time to physically or mentally prepare for your Babytism. Eleven days is just about enough time to relax on holiday, so having 11 days to prepare for your life changing forever is not a lot of time. I think that my fellow big and I were running on adrenaline for a few days, and we had to be careful about going mad with the old shopping. What do you buy? How much do you buy? Clothes are easy, they are like grown-up clothes but tiny. But, when we go into the niche part of buying for babies, it becomes massively overwhelming. There are so many nappies, creams, milks, beddings, wipes, etc. which ones do you get? Fortunately, when we were with Alice and Frank before they went on their hols, we wrote a list of 'must haves when you have a teeny wee human.'

This was our list: -
- Anbesol (not to be mistaken for Anusol)
- Metanium (white and yellow: a little goes a long long way)
- Size 1 nappies (who knew that all size 1 nappies are different sizes? Sainsbury's nappies are tiny compared to pampers)
- MAM Anti-colic bottles
- Tommee Tipee perfect bottle prep (the teasmaid of baby bottles)
- A steriliser
- Nappy changing mat
- Baby towels
- Fitted sheets for cots (they are tiny and as difficult to put on as a king sized bed
- And obviously, clothes

When we went through transition we were going through the 'Hottest Summer on record....EVER!' so we had to be super prepared and therefore purchased a pram fan (a wonderous thing that you can pivot to blow on yourself and dry off the slightly damp brow you can acquire when walking in 33 degree heat) and a UVA pop-up tent to protect the teeny wee human from the sun's rays.

The eleven days Baby A, Frank and Alice were on their hols went with surprising speed, but we also felt as though it took its time. Eleven days passed, and we arrived at Father's Day 2018 aka Transition, in five days Baby A would be coming home with us, her soon to be Bigs.

During transition you spend your time at your teeny wee human's foster carers home, shadowing their day, learning routines, and for us, learning how to do all the things we had no idea how to do. Alice was amazing! She showed us and supported us through our first nappy change/ poop explosion. She taught us how to prepare formula, and showed us how to put clothes onto the teeny wee human as we found the arms terrifying: what if we managed to snap one off whilst trying to get one into the army hole????

We felt quite privileged to spend time with Frank and Alice during our transition. It was so evident that being foster carers was not their 'job' but their way of life. Alice told us that they love their foster children as if they were their own children, which was evident in how they looked after Baby A and the other child they were fostering during our time in transition. They told us that even though they loved their foster children, their job was complete when they saw them find their parents and their forever family: that moment when child and Big met for the first time made the heartache of saying goodbye worth it.

The last two days of transition are, to put simply, weird! The penultimate day of transition you go to the foster carer's home and collect your teeny wee human and take them to your home and spend the day in what will become their home. For us, it was an opportunity for my Bigs and my American Aunty who was over in the UK on holiday to meet our teeny wee human. It was a hallmark moment. My dad cried, and then my mum cried, and then my Aunt followed suit. They had watched us wait and hoop jump to become a family, and we were now 24 hours and a thousand more hoops and hurdles to overcome until we got to forever, but we were there with our teeny wee human on the precipice of forever.

At the end of this penultimate day, you take the teeny wee human back to the foster carer's home and leave for the last time, empty handed, sans child. I couldn't tell you what we did that night, but I will assume that we went for an Indian meal (as it sustains our life lol).

The last day is full of emotion.

We woke up early, got ready, knowing that we would be bringing home our teeny wee human but we would also be saying goodbye to our teeny wee human's foster carers who we have grown so fond of over such a short period of time.

When we arrived at the house of Frank and Alice, Baby A's family finder was there to supervise the 'hand over', to take a photograph of the 5 of us together, and to let us know when we would expect our first social worker visit, as now we were officially Baby A's foster-to-adopt parents. People we were not supposed to be called mum and dad until the placement order was made, but who social services called mum and dad from the moment we saw our little girl because it was meant to be, it was just when not if. We were there for less than an hour before we left with our teeny wee human in her baby carrier contraption. My fellow Big and I crossed the road feeling as though the stabilisers had been ripped from us, but we were ready. We drove the 8 miles home like we had won the lottery (but sensible and in control).

You think you will remember that first day, but you don't. You remember the feeling leaving the foster carer's home for the last time, but you don't know what you did when you got home because for the first hours, days, weeks and months, the moments flow into the next like a blur. You can pick out moments but not individual days.

My fellow Big being self-employed is not entitled to paternity leave or any form of subsidy because…he is self-employed, so if he doesn't work then he doesn't get paid, and as he had lost nearly £8000 during the adoption training and transition, he had to go to work as soon as Baby A came home because he was embracing the responsbility that was now on his shoulders: he was, and is a Dad, so being the responsible person he is he went back to work, and this was inspite of the social workers wanting him to take another month off work, which is also known as loose the opportunity to earn £4000, in spite of them being clenched about him being self employed.

So, the day after our Teeny Wee Human moved home, I was flying solo from 7.30am – 4pm. Objective was to feed, change and survive until my fellow big came home and we could parent/ figure this stuff out together.

We had now been well and truly dropped into the middle of the parenting storm, it was the birth of our Babytism.

And so, the Babytism begins…

The Babytism of Fire

Chapter 4 *
Never wake a sleeping baby! Never!

We can't remember what we did during that first day when the teeny wee human came home, but we can remember the first night. We were lucky that Alice had a routine that our Teeny Wee Human followed, and all we needed to do was to follow it.

We were told that she would go to sleep around 5.30pm and then she would wake about 10pm and would need feeding. Like clockwork she went to sleep when we were expecting her to, and then we waited... and waited... and waited for her to wake to have her bottle. 10pm came and went. We were pooped and wanted to go to bed, but we were aware that she hadn't eaten.

Now, we have all heard the phrase 'never wake a sleeping baby!' and I think many people would wonder 'why?'... well, let our experience be your warning to waking the sleeping infant.

In our naivity/ stupidness, we decided that we should wake the teeny wee human because a) she would be hungry b) she would need a new nappy and c) she would be over-joyed that we had considered this and woke her up in order to rectify this. WRONG!!!!

Upon her little eyes fluttering open, she started to wail as if the world was ending. We changed her and fed her mid-gasps of hysteria, upon completion of our tasks I picked her up to comfort her and she projectile vommited all over me and down my top. As most people who have had a small human puke on them, there is nothing more unsettling than having puke in the cup of your brassier. Slightly repulsed and impressed, I passed the crying teeny wee human to my fellow big who had escaped the chunderful moment that I had just experienced.

This moment, and dumb-ass decision making felt as though it lasted a lifetime but in reality she was back asleep within 30 minutes.

Because we are smart humans we learnt form this experience, and the following night, night number 2, we did not wake the sleeping teeny wee human. We did however watch the clock hit 10pm again. My fellow big said 'she wont be asleep much longer, I shall stay up until she wakes and feed her. Then I shall come to bed. You go and sleep!' Again, oh how wrong we were. It was 2am before she decided to rouse and need feeding. Thankfully my fellow big bigged it up for the two of us and I was able to sleep – a woman needs 8 hours at least to function during the day.

After the debacle of night 1 and night 2, it was a pearl of wisdom and joy from an old school friend of mine who said 'dream feed'…and dream feed we did! The teeny wee human from night 3 did not awake in the night as a hungry Harry, she slept through until the morning. Result!

Bigs 'vs' teeny wee humans... Sleeping!

Well like many parents the world over, when the teeny wee bundle of joy joins the household your ability to sleep stops and it becomes a battle of wills...

Night No#1

1st night with teeny tot in the house. Baby - 1. Adults - 0.
I wouldn't mind she slept, I just freaked out everytime she moved. I must get better at the not panicking, baby's move.

Night No#2

2nd night with teeny wee human and I think we have levelled the score... Baby - 1: adults - 1. That is because:-
She slept from 7.30pm to 2.30am; 3am to 7.30am
Mason pulled a major man-dult card and took care of the feed like the legend that he is, whilst I searched for my big girl pants as I was too scared to do it.

Night No#3

The Emmy for the best new big human to a teeny wee human goes to Mason ☐ he managed to dream feed teeny wee human with reflux that makes the Exorcist look like a tactile chunder at 2.30am without a) waking said teeny wee human, and b) avoiding apocalyptic reflux... I was too worried about a) reflux-gate 2018 b) waking the sleeping human.

So night 3...asleep at 9.15pm awake 6.07am
PLUS Mason has allowed me to sleep for another two hours because I was kept awake by the teeny wee human's very loud squeaking due to a very floppy larynx.
What I've learnt after night 3:-
* my husband is bloody amazing and I am a very lucky girl
* I need to find my big girl pants so I can dream feed said tiny wee human
* parenthood is a) teamwork b) takes a village
* I have so much respect for solo bigs to teeny wee humans, I am in awe of you. You are amazing!

Night No#4

So, we're getting ready to embark on night 4 of the Masons vs the teeny wee human... So far, I have tried on my big girl pants and managed to feed her without waking her up completely (yay me! I deserve a medal) but then I think the elastic broken because then a feared the 'putting her down as I may wake her'. Luckily my right arm aka Mason twanged the elastic told me to man up, and down the teeny wee human went and we have a still sleeping teeny wee human. Hurrah!
This afternoon a free kick was awarded to the teeny wee human and we were given a 6 place grid penalty for 'not being able to make the crying stop in spite of feeding, changing, napping, cuddling, repeat'... What did I learn:
* trapped wind sucks even when it isn't my own
* napping for adults is a joy and I've spend 37 years hating them
* teeny wee human nails are like razor blades and they don't half smart when they dig in to sunburnt flesh.
Wish us luck... Mason is owning the dream feed, I have faulty big girl pants and we're hoping that we too will sleep like a teeny wee human rather than a restless big one.

Night 4 was definitely a photo finish... We all tried our hardest, but on the night it just wasn't completely in our control. It was all down to timing. Tiny wee human made an excellent start after an afternoon of being a complete diva, throwing major tantrums at life - resulting in the adults being clueless in finding a solution, after some last minute discussions we concluded a) teeny wee human was hot b) in spite of hotness she wanted to be in her body suit and not just her nappy: the girl has standards c) she enjoys being carried up and down stairs.
Teeny wee human hit the hay at 7.30pm with food in her belly and a clean nappy. This big human managed to dream feed her at 9.30pm with a dodgy big girl pant

elastic put her down and she continued to sleep... Win! I am accepting medals and certificates for my achievement. Roll on bed time for the adults and we too, for the first time since teeny wee human moved in, slept ☐

1am comes round and teeny wee human is fed - dream style. It was all going well when the poonarmi to end all poonarmis happened and the eyes pinged open and the tears started. Step in Mason who dealt with said nappy trauma and teeny wee human returned to her state of previous slumber, and we adults managed this too.... Do I hear applause?!?

Roll of 5.05am and the little tinker awakes demanding food immediately. So this big human steps up to bat, food is administered, sleep is returned at 6am and she is still pushing out the ☐ now.... I don't know if this is good but I'm taking it. Bottles are sterilised, I've hit the cereal and I am now putting together charts to try to get to the crux of routine because at the moment teeny wee human is just being a diva... Lucky she is adorable and squeaks ☐

Night No#5

Well night 5 was simply thrilling, sitting on the edge of your seat kinda stuff, and I think it ended 1 up for the bigs ... Teeny wee human went to bed at about 8pm and was eyes closed sending up the ☐ by 8.30pm - WIN! Mason and I then woke at 3am with no shrieking teeny wee human but one who had managed to shuffle herself around 180 and to the bottom of the crib. Start dream sleep and teeny wee human slept until 5.45am woke for a snack and the returned to the land of nod until 7.45am. We're going into the home stretch of the end of week one optimistic that we can do this in spite of diva moments, projectile vomit and poo... Oh the poo!

Night No#6

Well after a day that made Panama's world cup performance look worthy of the World Cup itself, last night we pulled it back and had another delightful evening thanks to the teeny wee human's love of sleep. Bed at 8.30pm dream fed at 3.30am and the up at 6.50am. I'm not going to lie, as a big who herself loves sleep I would be appreciative if another 45minutes kip, but I cant complain.
Lessons learnt:
* when I teeny wee human is being a diva you can feel like a bag of poo, but then they sneeze and everything is OK with the world
* snot is horrible if you don't have the ability to blow your nose or to snot it out like a highly paid footballer with no manners.

* we have nearly survived the last week after being dropped into the eye of a storm without a parachute, safety net or a pair of roller skates.

Tonight, we embark on night number 7 - one whole week since our teen wee human flipped our upside down and inside out.

Night No. 7 and I found my big girl pants

Since our teeny wee human dropped into our world, I seemed to have lost all my big girl pants as I've relied on Mason to do the night feeds whilst I watch on in awe of the man who can feed a sleeping baby without drowning them. So, I have been like Sunderland FC: I show up, but do nothing once I'm there lol!

Flash forward 7 nights, and Mason needing to get up at silly o'clock for work, I donned the big girl pants and took ownership of the night feed of our gripey, snoofly and snotty teeny wee human (a more challenging evening I may add) and I did it. I FED THE BABY! And she stayed ASLEEP.

Not only did my newly found big girl pants come in handy for the night feed, but I believe that they supported me through 'the nappy change'. I feel at this point is that I should share my napping experiences to date… I changed my 1st one when we met our teeny wee human a little over a week ago. I digress… This morning, big girl pants, nappy… Oh lord! It was all going smoothly, like planned. Unstick nappy, legs up – hers not mine, wet wipe at the ready and the poo… It came from nowhere and shot across the changing table with the force of jumping on a mustard packet. Shocked, and repulsed, I reacted: dodged, used the wipe and fresh nappy as protection. Crisis averted. Big girl pants – win!

So, 7 nights in I feel like I have achieved a lot… I've big girled up. I've been puked on (think the Exorcist but with more gusto), mastered supporting a night feed, now I've done the night feed too! And I have dodged a poo missile and changed a poonado without puking myself.

We move on from week one, but the baby-tism continues… Apparently next week is a 'wonder week'??? I'm wondering what that is.

Chapter 5
And so, the visits begin; one social worker to another

The one constant you have in your life when you go through adoption are social workers. They become a weekly regular (a little bit like Last of the Summer Wine in the 80s) throughout stage 2, but once you get placed with a teeny wee human, they continue to fill their regular slot and become so familiar with your home that they don't only know where the loo is, they also know where you keep you mugs and coffee.

Our teeny wee human moved home on the Thursday, and on the Friday the visits began. This is where I think the biggest difference is between birthing your own human and finding one (for want of a better phrase) through adoption. If you birth your own human no one visits and checks in on you on a weekly basis whereby you have to look like you a) have a clue and b) have your shit together.

I remember that first visit well. I had managed to have a shower (victory), apply my eye liner, and brush my teeth, so I thought I was doing pretty well…but from that point the idea of putting the small human down was quite worrying, so I didn't. I was applying with a degree of efficiency: nappy, feed, nap, and repeat, and then Doris came round. I hadn't eaten. I hadn't had a cup of coffee. I was holding it together by a thread. I was flying solo for the first time in a completely new situation, floating through the eye of the storm, and I was expected to look like I had it together, that I knew what I was doing and to talk about how things were going. I honestly don't think I could have spelt my somewhat lengthy name at that point, let alone sound like I had a clue, yet I did.

Doris came round to see how we were 'attaching', settling in and getting on as a family, as well as managing the requirements of being FFA adopters, medical appointments, poop and vom, on a weekly basis for two months, and then on a fortnightly visit for the next two months, and then monthly for the following two months.

Not only did we have our social worker visit, we also had our teeny wee human's social worker visit to assess how she was developing and getting on, because ultimately, they have to be 100% certain that they had made the right choice of choosing us to be the Bigs to the teeny wee human they were in charge and responsible for.

Don't get me wrong having a weekly, fortnightly, and monthly visit was annoying and at times something you felt like actively rolling your eyes at, but in a weird way it was supportive whilst being judgemental at the same time.

At times we completely disagreed with our social worker, and certainly at the situations we were expected to put our teeny wee human and ourselves in because it was immoral, but I have to give Doris her due, she took our criticism of the system with two barrels and did not judge us negatively for it. But for so many adopters and FFA adopters they are too afraid to say how they feel to social workers out of fear of repercussions, however we feel that we have a moral duty to hold social services to account for the poor choices they make at times in the name of it 'being in the best interest of the child' when it clearly is not.

'There's no right, there's no wrong, there's only popular opinion' **Twelve Monkeys**

We have a winner... And it's me!

Step aside 4th place - it's coming home - get paid too much - England International football team (really, I'm proud of the accomplishment of the team: way to bring a country together... This morning though, I'm reigning supreme and they can sing Oasis to me ☐) for I have had my big girl pants on all night, and the elastic was super reinforced and mighty.

It all started at 9.26pm (precision is key)... "I've got the bottles" and off I tootle up the apples and pears thinking my fellow big would be behind with his feeding of teeny wee human strength... Alas he was not, so I scooped said sleeping teeny wee human from her pit of slumber and fed... Not drown... Fed the teeny wee human... And not just a whistle wetting, pretty much 4oz! Teeny wee human continued to knock out the zzzz.

Fellow big was super pooped after a long tiring week, holding the Fort one evening, and being man of super strength (emotionally) whilst the teeny wee human had her jabs and cried proper tears... So he hit the hay sending up the zzzz.... I was surrounded by slumber, so I too hit the hay.

The Babytism of Fire

Flash forward to 2.36am, teeny wee human becomes restless in her slumber. I stir, big girl pants at the ready. I glance at my fellow big who is swaddled in sleep, so I get the bottle, scoop sleeping teeny wee human and again, I feed, not drown the teeny wee human. It was going swimmingly until poo! The eyes of the teeny wee human open, I panic, utter words of reassurance, and we have NO TEARS! (hers or mine) win!

Keeping calm, I take teeny wee human to the nursery, change the expoosion, reswaddle (1/2), and continue to feed. The fellow big is still pushing out zzzz, I'm flying solo... I am Top Gun. Teeny wee human starts to fuss, I pop her back into the pit if sleep and.... Sparko!

Which brings me to this morning. 6am, restless teeny wee human. I go downstairs, make her medication, prepare a bottle. Return to the land of rest (them, not me) scoop the teeny wee human up, give her medication, pop in the dummy and she is still sparko.... Now I await my feeding duty. It's now 6.50am and I have a sleeping teeny wee human and fellow big. I'm awake and would kill for a starbucks, but I think I've been a winner! And I believe it has ended 5 - 1 to me...Pass me my medal ☐

Chapter 6
Living with uncertainty

In the 'Days of Yore' women wore girdles which not only synched in the waist and made your bulgy bits look all womanly and attractive, they also offered you support, and throughout the whole adoption process you have various people who become your metaphorical girdle: they lift you up and offer you the support you need. For us, support has not been family parachuting in to 'babysit' or have people come round and 'give us a breather', it has been those folk who have invited us for coffee, carried on talking to us as adults whilst we are drenched in puke, or those people who have been on the end of the phone and listened to us talk all things baby without so much as a 'how are you?'. One of the things that can make you feel the need for a girdle whilst going through the adoption process, certainly as FFA adopters is uncertainty.

That word 'uncertainty' is flung around like a mound of cow-shit in a cowpat throwing competition: it takes flight, but no one knows where exactly it will land once it hits the air. The term 'uncertainty' in itself presents just that – uncertainty. Now, my fellow Big and I were not put off by this concept much to social services surprise, because in our minds, if we had birthed our own human what we would get would be in the lap of the Gods anyway so why is a human being born from the body of someone else any more uncertain? Yes, we don't know what the environmental factors are, but do they really matter????

As FFA adopters (more so that 'straight-forward' adopters) the one thing you are told again and again, is that there is uncertainty. Uncertainty in how your teeny wee human will develop: they may have been exposed to all sorts of things in vitro and therefore have a huge question mark hanging over their head – according to social services, not necessarily the medical professionals you speak to. You don't just live with medical and developmental uncertainty – for us this was academic and didn't matter – you live with the greater uncertainty, and that is that at any point your teeny wee human could be taken from you and returned to their natural habitat.

When you get approved as FFA adopters you are asked how you would deal with it if the teeny wee human you had bonded with was returned to their birth humans, and I remember giving the most Miss World answer we could have…and we meant it. We said that it would break our hearts if our teeny wee human went back to their birth humans, but we would be happy in the fact that we had given her a positive start in life, shown her love without condition, and that would be Ok with us. But in spite of that the prospect of it is pretty gut wrenching and hangs perpetually over your heads until you get your final order.

In the world of adoption and matching, you are presented with a whole chunk of information about your teeny wee human at various points in the process. If you go through 'straight-forward' adoption you will have access to a document called a CPR prior to being matched with your child. A CPR is the Child's Permanence Report which is a lengthy document cataloguing the history of the birth humans, encounters with the law and social services, any birth siblings and what has happened to them, medical issues of the birth humans and a whole load of other information that social services believe to be the 'history' of the child you adopting: they call it 'information that will form your child's life story work' and information that could inform your decision to proceed with the adoption of the teeny wee human. In the world of FFA you do not get access to this information until a lot further down the line, and at the point in which you get this information, you don't really care about what it says as that teeny wee human is yours: they are your child – emotionally, but not yet legally.

Our teeny wee human came to us with a Protection Order and a Section 21 Care Order, which meant that for her own safety she was award of the state – the irony of this is that even though it is down to social services to act in the interest of the child, the responsibility is shared with the birth parents who have been deemed as 'unfit' to parent. At this point in an FFA procedure the whole network within the birth families are investigated and explored as being potential matches for the teeny wee human, but the teeny wee human has been placed with FFA adopters because social services are 95% certain that there is no one suitable in the birth network and that the judge will agree that adoption is the best option for the teeny wee human to thrive and be happy.

Even though you have some confidence from social services you go through the days, weeks and months, when you fall even more in love with your teeny wee human, holding your breath because there is no such thing as certain until the fat lady sings...It is only once the Placement Order is made do you have some indication of certainty and outcome, but it still isn't definite. A Placement Order means that the judge overseeing the case believes that adoption is in the best interest of the child and therefore they are officially able to be 'put up for adoption'.

For us, by the time we had our Placement Order our teeny wee human had been living with us for nearly 2 months, we had been there when her birth was registered, held her when she had her vaccinations and blood tests. We had become amateur masters at dealing with chronic reflux, and I had revived her when she had temporarily stopped breathing. The day we received our Placement Order, it was in actual fact the day of her Resolution Hearing which is when any evidence is presented to the court by the social workers to support adoption or the birth family to argue it. Our Resolution Hearing turned into the Placement Order which meant that we could start to breathe out a little more and the swinging axe slowed down just a little.

Because Placement Order meant that as FFA adopters we were the people book marked to adopt our teeny wee human we now had to be 'matched' to our teeny wee human by social services. This was our green mile. This was more nerve-wracking than adoption panel because we were now invested, committed and besotted with our teeny wee human. We were asked questions like 'why did we want to adopt our teeny wee human?', 'what could we offer her as parents?', 'how do we cope with her reflux?' This is also another part of the process whereby 'adoption' and 'FFA' have not caught up with each other. In 'straightforward' adoptions you are matched before you meet your teeny wee human and before they move home to you. With FFA, you are matched to your teeny wee human once they have been living with you for a while and after the Placement Order has been made, so you have formed a family by this point and theoretically the matching panel could decide that you are not the right parents for your teeny wee human.

We remember leaving the matching panel interview and sitting in an interview room in social services HQ and waiting for only 10 minutes, but those 10 minutes felt like 10 hours. We couldn't think of any reason why they could argue against us being Bigs to our teeny wee human, but sometimes the world can be cruel, and we weren't going to count our chickens, not until that fat bird started singing. When our social workers and family finder, alongside the panel chair walked into the room I think my fellow big and I took a deep breath…and then we heard the words 'we all agreed that you should be Bigs to our teeny wee human and that they felt as though we had already shown that we will act in the best interest of her'.

The uncertainty falls away like a checklist completed as time passes, but as time passes the stakes get higher. By matching you have already checked off: -
- ✓ Finding teeny wee human/ being found for teeny wee human
- ✓ Panicking and shopping
- ✓ Transition
- ✓ Moving home
- ✓ Resolution Hearing
- ✓ Placement Order

- ✓ Matching Panel

With the obviously interim check-offs of
- ✓ Master of Puke
- ✓ Master of Poo
- ✓ Master of arms
- ✓ Master of bathtime
- ✓ Master of brushing your teeth whilst holding your baby and making a cup of coffee

And obviously,
- ✓ Master of the Universe

But you still have the big ones to get a tick next to.
- ✓ Directions Hearing
- ✓ Final Hearing
- ✓ Celebration Hearing

The last three things come in quick succession of each other but the stark reality that you are way down the list of 'significant people' becomes even more obvious. The Directions Hearing is where the court will give 'direction' (clue in the title) as to what is needed in order for the final hearing to happen. As prospective adopters you do not attend any court hearing until the celebration hearing because the birth humans are invited to court and are able to contest the adoption. They are able to appeal even once the judge has given the Adoption Order at the Final Hearing. They are able to appeal up to 21 days after the Final Hearing. So even once you are mum and dad, by law, you don't get your 100% certainty until the Judge gives your teeny wee human a lovely teddy bear at the Celebration Hearing and looks you in the face and says that you are a family...finally.

Sometimes you just need a girdle.

When you go through adoption you have to present your 'eco-map' of support, and we felt really lucky that we could say that we could call someone in any time zone and get support, to which we were told was great but who was physically close to us?

Mason and I have always been each other's girdle of support and with that we have not sought close friendships with people beyond those we already have... Those friends are scattered across the globe and have been our friends for years. As a result we place greater value in emotional support which we get in spades from our friends.

However, since teeny wee human parachuted into our lives we have found that we have girdles in places we didn't know. It means a lot when people genuinely ask how you are, offer to babysit, to pop round for coffee or to give you reassurances that you are doing a good job.

At times it is tough, especially when the teeny wee human wails for 6 hours straight and shredded my resilience and nerve which brought me to the brink of tears. It has been comforting to know that when I needed it, I had a choice of girdles to support me and get me back into shape.

The girdles amongst you... Thank you!

Chapter 7
'Close encounters of the third kind' Contact

One of the strangest, and possibly most stressful moment as Foster to Adopters is the idea that you may have to facilitate contact. You are 'prepared' for it in a way, but the reality is, taking your child to spend time with their birth humans is something that fills you with dread. Throughout the process you are asked about how you would cope, what strategies would you employ during this time: and like any normal person we came up with 'go to B&Q', 'take a stroll round Tesco', 'go for a walk'…do something to de-stress.

We were lucky and as FFA adopters we didn't have to facilitate regular contact with the birth humans – which was a huge sigh of relief. There is nothing quite like taking your child to see their birth humans to remind you that you are the bottom of the pile, you mean nothing in the grand scheme of the social care system, and that apparently 'it is for the best interest of the child' (when we all know that it isn't).

But, even though we didn't have to facilitate daily or weekly contact, we did have to facilitate one contact with one of the birth humans (I am reluctant to say father or mother because they lost the right to that title when they failed to be a parent; those labels are sacred, and they have never been our teeny wee human's mother or father). It was awful.

We were told to write a letter to the human about our teeny wee human's well-being, provide a photograph, not to feed her or change her because this would provide evidence as to whether they were prepared to meet her needs. The day came, and we felt sick. For a few hours we were going to hand our teeny wee human over to her social worker and be taken, in a controlled environment, to spend time with a complete stranger: someone she did not know and whom she had never met. During that time, the social worker would be assessing their ability to parent. A time when we were not with her. The only thing we could do was to kill time in a shop yards from where they were and wait for the phone to ring to say that they were out… two hours lasted a life time.

When we were finally reunited with our teeny wee human, we were told that the birth human was very loving towards her, but reluctantly fed her, and drew the line at changing her nappy leaving it to the social worker to do it.

We were very lucky with the teeny wee human's social worker, as she was very cognisant about how the process was making us feel, in particular how this moment in time was making my fellow big, our teeny wee human's dad, feel. She made the point of telling us that we were her parents and that we were the people our teeny wee human looked for. It made us feel better, but it didn't make the situation any easier.

That day was so incredibly challenging for us, but it was just another moment in the process that reminds you that you have to be resilient and stead-fast in what you think, feel and believe. Yes, we were having to facilitate contact. Yes, it is immoral and in no way 'in the best interest of the child' – certainly not for a baby. But, you do what you have to do because you are that teeny wee human's parents in waiting and if that means you have to lie down on a bed of nails whilst being covered in fire ants and being twanged with elastic bands, you pull your big girl pants all the way up and you do it. Then when the moment is past, you talk to your fellow big about your feelings, you have a coffee and a doughnut, and you put it in the 'done' box and try not to dwell on it. You also make sure that you explain to your social worker, whether they like the words that fall out of your mouth or not, what the experience was like and how you felt about it: and give Doris her due, she took it both barrels that day and acknowledged that taking a baby to meet a complete stranger is immoral and wrong, and in no way in the best interest of the child.

And it was everywhere...

For some reason when you become a parent you also gain an accute (not to be mistaken with 'a cute') obsession with poo: when did they last poo? How much was there? Should you be worried? How many poos? The list is endless.

Now, don't get me wrong, I love a good poo joke like the next person but the poo of a teeny wee human is nothing to be laughed at (even though they may have a giggle at your expense when you place them on the changing mat because they know what they are making you deal with).

This week our teeny wee human has been troubled with traumatic farts and absent poos, that is until this weekend. It is a good job I am not squeamish because if I was the poor mite would have been dealing with a face full of vomit as well as a warm and unpleasant nappy.

Since our teeny wee human turned our two into a three, we have gone from 'I've never changed a nappy' into a nappy in seconds, in the dark, whilst half asleep masters - step aside Yoda this is our turf! And we have dealt with poonarmis, poonados, but today we (I say we... It was all me, with a little help from my mothership) dealt with a nappy apoocalypse: it was everywhere! In the nappy. Out the nappy. And then when cleaning up the teeny wee human she decided to lay her leg in it. It was an unweilding beast of poo. The only saving grace was we didn't have a repeat experience of the flying poo missile.

Several baby wipes later, the apoocalypse was dealt with and the teeny wee human was peeled out of her poo-traumatised outfit, fitted with a fresh baby outfit and ready to take the world by storm.

Prior to having a teeny wee human many things worried me: arms, heads and nappies. I think we've now got these little gems sorted.

Chapter 8
Meet the parents

Gone are the days where total anonymity is involved in the wonderful world of adoption. For some reason unbeknownst to us, the social care system is encouraging more and more the notion of 'openness' – whether it is right or wrong, I don't know. The 'openness' is not a Disney Movie, lets all be friends and live like the Brady Bunch in a beautiful blended family of wonderfulness, it is a bit darker than that.

If there are birth siblings, you may or may not be encouraged or 'voluntold' to have contact with them once or twice a year. This could be vis-à-vis depending on whether it is 'best for the children' and usually the case whereby the children are older, have an established relationship but have been placed for adoption separately. The same may apply for aunties, uncles, and grand-parents.

In all cases, you are expected to 'maintain letter box contact' with birth siblings and parents. This is where you write a letter to the birth humans, a newsy letter, letting them know how your child is getting on. It goes to social services and then you may or may not get a reply from the birth humans. Social services try to encourage the child to be a part of this process when they are older and are able to understand the complex tapestry that is their birth past. This is something I think is madness; how to create the potential for identity and belonging issues in a child and then an adult – as an adult it would be hard to comprehend, as a child it is going to be mind-blowing. I fear that too often we try to project adult ideals and responses to children and forget that they are children and see the world differently to us, and rightly so.

With regards to the birth humans, prior to the Adoption Order being made, it is encouraged for you to meet one or both of them. Now, if you have seen 'Meet the Parents' with Ben Stiller and Rober Di Niro, you will know that meeting parents can be quite stressful. It isn't quite the same obviously, as you have no intention of dating or marrying the person you are about to meet, you know of them based on the information you have received on them from social services and there is a strong possibility that you won't like them.

We always said that we would do what was expected of us and meeting the birth human was something neither of us wanted to do, but it is something both of us did do because we said we would. We didn't know what to expect. We felt sick. We didn't have anything to ask him, because he didn't know our daughter and aside from biology, he had contributed nothing to her. We didn't care what his favourite colour was. We didn't care what musical tastes he had.

I think that this is one aspect, having spoken to other adopters, that unifies us. We don't want to meet them, but we do, and in a peculiar way we all find it positive. For us the positivity came because we got to see what he looked like, gave assurances – even though we didn't have to – that our daughter would be loved and looked after without question, and that we could say that we did it because we always said we would. We did get the added bonus that he gave his 'blessing' for want of a better word to the court and that he would not object to us adopting her. For us, he was no longer a name on a page, he was human, and I guess humanising rather than demonising the birth humans for us gives us peace – I guess.

I would say by far and away that meeting the parents was the hardest part of the adoption process (outside of the waiting and unknowns). It is something that you can't prepare yourself for, so you just have to go with it, with sweaty hands and a pit in your stomach. But you get through it, you move on and it is something else that can go in the 'done' box whether you choose to give it air space or head space afterwards, that is your choice.

Chapter 9
One small step for us... one giant leap to forever: placement order

The whole adoption process, whether 'straight-forward' adoption or FFA, is a series of small steps. If you are lucky all the steps that you take will be in the same direction: forward. If you are really unlucky the step that you have to take may be over a small hurdle or a fast-moving river that you have to navigate in order to get onto the other side. In the world of adoption, adoption cannot happen unless you get a little thing called a Placement Order.

A Placement Order in the legal bit whereby the judge has viewed and reviewed all the evidence and has decided that the child should be 'put up' for adoption and social services can start to look for the teeny human's forever family.

In the case of FFA the Placement Order has not been made when the teeny human moves home, they are just pretty certain that one will be given, so they look for the forever family, place the wee human with them, and then hope the Placement Order is made. Until the Placement Order is made you live with a swinging axe over your head and the threat that at any point the axe could cut through the rope and the teeny wee human who you have given your home to, your heart to, and who you view as being your teeny wee human could be returned to a human within their natural habitat.

Our teeny wee human had been living with us for 1 month and 17 days, or 6 weeks and 5days, or 47 days, or 1128 hours when we got notice that the Placement Order had been made. Now, in the grand scheme of things that doesn't seem like a long period of time, but what you have to understand is that everything within our journey took place within the middle of a tornado – it happened so quickly that the opportunity to process and do anything other than 'go with it' was not an option. During those 1128 hours we had been to Drs, hospitals, contact and meeting of the birth human; we had learned to become accustomed to chronic reflux, held her whilst she screamed in pain, soothed her whilst she was having an endoscopy, and I had revived her when she had stopped breathing and was unconscious, all whilst being supervised, visited and judged as to whether or not we were the right people to be the Bigs to our teeny wee human.

The Placement Order marked the first moment when we could start to unclench our butt cheeks and start to slowly yet cautiously breathe out.

I remember my fellow Big speaking to our teeny wee human's social worker and saying I know that the Placement Order has been made but we know that doesn't mean we can breathe out completely yet: she said that it would be over her dead body – or something to that effect. Her positivity gave us reassurance, but we still weren't prepared to breathe out completely until the Adoption Order was made, but that wouldn't be for another 137 days.

Chapter 10
...And it's a match: matching panel

From a young age you learn that matching two pairs is a good thing: snap, poker…You learn that finding two of a kind wins the game. The role of the family finder is to find two of a kind – a forever family. When it comes to 'straight-forward' adoption the matching is done before the teeny wee human moves home. In the world of FFA the formal matching is not done until the Placement Order has been made.

But what is matching?

Once the family finder and all the social workers involved have looked at all the necessary Permanence Reports, and you as prospective Bigs have agreed that you would like to pursue a match with a teeny wee human, you are put in front of a matching panel. Matching panel is a group of 8 people who have different experiences and backgrounds within the world of adoption and it is their job to question prospective adopters about their desire to parent the teeny wee human they are seeking a match to, and ultimately decide as to whether or not they feel that you will make good Bigs to the teeny wee human.

When we went to matching panel, our teeny wee human had been with us for 3 months near enough to the day…imagine if you had birthed your own human and at 3 months a group of strangers had to decided whether or not that wee human was to stay with you and be yours. Imagine that the only thing they knew about you was what they had read by your social workers and what you were going to say in the next 40 minutes.

Walking into matching panel was like entering the twilight zone. We were flanked by our social workers and had 7 expectant faces looking at us, and one chap who decided to take the opportunity to have a nap. We sat there with sweaty hands (and shins. I have, for some reason, developed the ability to get sweaty shins when nervous) and waited for the first question and then the next, and the next, and the next, until it was over, and we got to walk our green mile.

These were our questions, and imagine how you would be able to answer them (well the ones that are not specific to us):-

- Why do you want to parent your teeny wee human?
- What do you have to offer as a parent?
- How will you teach your teeny wee human about their history, how they became your child?
- How do you cope with their medical condition?
  (Now this question got a lot of gasps as I explained that I had revived our teeny wee human, and you just have to deal with their medical conditions because that is your job as a parent.)
- Why did I decide to write my blog?

When we left the room and were ushered into the waiting room of concrete and high ceilings, my fellow Big and I waited and waited, not quite knowing what to do with ourselves. We had just gone in for a cuddle when the doors opened after a lifetime and our social worker and family finder, accompanied by the matching panel chair. I have no idea what fluff was said when they came back in, the only thing I can remember and heard properly was the fact that they had unanimously agreed that we should be the Bigs to our teeny wee human and that we had been her advocate and champion without question for the three months prior to that point.

As we left social services HQ feeling relieved. Doris said to us as we left whether we had our 'escape plan' of for any reason the world had gone mental and they had decided that we weren't a match…we hadn't, because we were confident that they would see we were the Bigs to our teeny wee human: she was ours, we were hers, we had waited nearly 9 years to find her.

Yet again, we found ourselves being able to breathe out a little bit more.

Poo on my leg 💩💩💩

Since getting our teeny wee human, the one thing that has both impressed and repulsed me is her pooing prowess. And today has been no exception!

After a little nap on the playmat, a fresh nappy instated, the feeding of the teeny wee human commenced. Queue the slightly flushed brow, a couple of traumatic farts and a bearing down onto the bottle to allow the poo eruption onto my knee to occur.

The thing I don't understand is that your poop evacuation hole points backwards, behind you... Why does the poop of a teeny wee human have the gravitation pull towards the emergency exit of the nappy: the leg hole????

This is the cause of me having to change my shorts. Not because the teeny wee human did the most epic poo that it deserved to be written down in history as being the poo to end all poos. No, it is because the poo escaped via the leg, eeked out her shorts, only to leave what can only be described as poo residue on my shorts. The teeny wee human pooped on my leg...both impressive and disgusting.

'Man-ecdote'

There is nothing quite like that moment when your fellow big returns to your bedroom clutching the teeny wee human with a quality baby changing 'manecdote'. Today's 'manedcote' went something a little like this...

I popped the teeny wee human on the changing mat and removed the wet, very wet nappy. I placed the nappy in the nappy bin (fabulous not faddy may I add) *and the bag holder would not spin. After fixing said bin, I turned around to see a smiling teeny wee human and what can only be described as pint sized portion of individual chicken korma for one. Lovely colour and pippiness for the poo officianados out there.*

After the exclamation of 'oh you would wouldn't you' as there was no nappy to catch the poop, upon closer inspection the chicken korma was still being dispensed with a toothpaste consistency. At which giggles started to erupt from the teeny wee human and the big.

Step in Sainsbury's size 2 nappy to wipe up and remove the korma from the changing mat and placed into the nappy bin which was once again broken.

I am very glad that I did not have to deal with today's poo-adventure... And I think we may have learnt that you always need a nappy to catch the surprise poos... As they may take you completely unawares: to quote Bruce Lee 'I do not (s) hit. It (s) hits all by itself' ... We're still laughing though.

Chapter 11
Living in limbo

I remember as a child going to the roller disco at our local recreation centre and the highlight of the night was when the limbo pole came out and you had to navigate your way under it whilst gliding across the overly polished floor without falling over…but if you did hit the deck, it was your goal, nay your duty to style out the battle you lost to gravity (also known as not crying like a toddler because falling over, no matter how old you are, makes you cry). Now, his story may seem somewhat out of place within the ramblings of a mad woman, but it is the perfect analogy as to how you feel once you get through the first hundred hurdles, you've matched and everyone agrees that you should be mum and dad to your teeny wee human but you have no rights, none whatsoever, thus leaving you in limbo, battling the low pole whilst trying not to hit the deck in a monumental heap of frustration and snot.

Fundamentally though, as soon as you hit limbo nothing changes. The only thing that has changed is that you have morphed from people who were a two, into a couple with a third who you have grown to love and adore, and who you would lay down your life for. You have become parents by heart but not by law…yet!

So how do you cope living in limbo? You just do. You go about your days in the weird non-routine that only puke and poop can provide you. You try to find classes to give you an excuse and a reason to leave the house and engage with other humans who have happened to have produced their own humans and become a little bit more mum and dad each day.

The main survival of limbo is laughing…not just the little 'ha ha' laugh which could be mistaken as a misplaced cough or a decisive move to mask a spontaneous fart in public. I mean a full on belly laugh at things that can only be inspired by the complete innocence of a teeny wee human, things like; laughing uncontrollably at the word poo (it is a classic), witnessing the playdoh poo travel across the changing mat and not having a clue as to what to do, or watching your teeny wee human become over joyed at the fact that they have discovered their feet and they can move independently of each other.

The thing is with limbo is that it bothers you more once you have been matched because you feel as though you are almost there, but in actual fact you still have a whole journey to travel. The reality is that you have been in limbo from the moment you found out that your teeny wee human was coming home. You haven't been able to go away for the weekend without announcing where, when and for how long for to the world and its aunt. You haven't even dreamed about going on an actual holiday (that is a complete lie because I have dreamt about boarding a plane for the last six months). You have had to report any minor blemish that may appear on your teeny wee humans face because they sprout razor blades from their fingers and you don't want Doris or Mavis to think that you have left your teeny wee human to frolic in broken glass that hasn't quite been worn down into sand yet. You have had to catalogue your days so that everything is recorded and reported as it indicates what type of parents you are: we have recorded everything aside from how long we shower or use the loo for on a daily basis for months. That doesn't change once you are matched, it continues until you get the piece of paper you have waited your whole life for the 'Adoption Order'.

We survived limbo: I managed to put my eyeliner on every day, without fail! Because I am, the words of Chandler Bing 'A strong independent woman.' And I have my fellow big propping me up when my eyeliner starts to resemble being applied in the dark.

Move over, I'm coming through…

It is official, the teeny wee human is attempting to move. It is adorable watching her scrunch her little legs up so her teeny tiny bottom is air bound, give it a little wiggle, and then launch herself forward, only for it to all go incredibly Pete Tong when the arms don't compliment the forward motion of the rear end.

It does make me think though, if the memory of trying to crawl remained with you there is no way on God's green earth that humans would be a species of perambulators… We would instead revert to being potatoes.

The one who is teeny and wee is a determined little munchkin. In spite of finding this movement lark so incredibly frustrating, she doesn't give up. Even when the frustration evokes a temporary throw down and boo hoo, she carries on. What a quality?! It's difficult but she'll be damned if she is bested by something as 'simple' as crawling. When she puts her mind to it she can shuffle across the floor, pivot and reach for what she wants.

But alas I think the bum wiggle crawl will be a skill she masters and abandons as she is desperate to walk. The teeny wee human has been comfortable weight bearing on her pins since she was 3 months and now she is standing (supported – she's not that advanced), bouncing and shifting weight from leg to leg.

As her big I am so keen on her becoming a mover because she will be able to start her mission of discovery of the world around her… Plus her moving = me not sat on my arse: it'll be fitness inducing lol! And item elevating.

She is still so teeny and wee, but she seems like a giant compared to how diddy she was, and moving will make her seem even bigger.

Chapter 12
Applying to court

As with many things within the adoption process, you glide up to it like a beautiful swan appearing like you know what is going on (a bit like the parenting malarkey) when in actual fact you have only a little bit of a clue, applying to court for the adoption order is no exception.

During one of our visits from Doris, I asked her about where we get the paperwork from to apply for court, and was told 'go on the internet' which was about as useful as a fart in a lift but it did mean that we could skip the waiting for someone else to give the paperwork to us bit... to be super formal and knowledgeable about it, the piece of paper is called a 'section 58'.

The form, like forms the world over, starts very simply with the bits that everyone can fill out without a degree in nuclear physics or a second job as a psychic. You have to start with your name and address, which obviously you will know because that bit is all about you. As the form goes on you have to add in information about your teeny wee human – again, other bits that you will know because they have become an extension of you, you are an expert in your teeny wee human and as such you've got that bit of the form in the bag. The form then goes on to cover the birth humans – information you have elicited from the social workers, in our case Mavis, and then you have to gain even more information, this time about any other children the birth humans have had and whether they had been part of the social care system too, if so, what their court details and order information was. If you have a social worker like Mavis who is on it like a car bonnet, that information came forth like the flowing waters of Babylon...if you don't, that bit of the form may be left a little bit empty.

Applying for court is the penultimate moment before your teeny wee human becomes legally yours and you are officially allowed to be dubbed 'mum and dad' by the world and its aunty. It is also the piece of paper whereby you can declare the name that will become your teeny wee human's for life. This is a huge responsibility! Social services won't allow you to change their first name because 'it may be the only thing their birth parents may have given them' (insert eye roll here), so you are left with choosing their middle name and, in our case, their last name (my fellow big and I, even though married have different last names as I am double-barrelled and have enough letters in it to put the actual alphabet to shame). We were pleased as punch when we learnt the name of our teeny wee human, our Baby A, because she wasn't a car, country, real name spelt wrong or a beverage – her name was beautiful, but we took the duty of choosing her middle name seriously. We wanted it to reflect her, be part of us and our journey in life, and to embody the spirit of who she will become, and as such she became 'The goddess of dawn, heavenly flower' and not 'noxious beverage, small crappy car aka Absinth Nova'.

That last page of the paperwork was, after all the fluff and blah blah that indicated the past that she had never experienced, the person she had been since she came home and will be the person she is until …well, forever!

Once you submit your paperwork to court, you do what you have become strangely accustomed to…waiting.

One Step Closer

The journey of an adopter is over-shadowed by moments that force an inhalation of breath. A pause. A hope. And then... Exhale.

For us, as foster-to-adopters, we have lived with the swinging guillotine over our necks for the last five and a half months: that possibility that someone could say *'your teeny wee human is going back to their birth family'*. And as much as we like to believe that we are stoical and pragmatic and we would have known that for all the months the teeny wee human was with us, she would have known unconditional love...If that had happened, I think our hearts would have broken into a million pieces.

That maybe. What if. It's possible. Keep it in the backs of your mind. Today, all that doubt has started to fall away, because today we were given our date for forever: the 20th December 2018.

So, today brings relief for us. It is the pee on stick moment magnified. The contractions. The harrowing pain of birth. The jubilation of meeting your teeny wee human for the first time. The leaving the hospital with your precious teeny human. Today, we found out that the 9 years of waiting, hoping and wanting, the what ifs, the maybes and the some days, will become one day, and one specific day.

However, like all steps in the process, I find myself conflicted. At no point did I want anyone to contest our adoption, to fight us for our daughter, but I can't help but feel a little sad that no one fought for her in the way we have from the day we learnt about her and knew she was ours. Ours of heart.

I know that in some point in the future our teeny wee human will have questions, but the one thing she will always know is that we loved her before we knew her, and that she was and is so very wanted, without condition.

When we were asked to be her bigs, we didn't know her name, we knew she was born and that she was in hospital fighting her own battle. We knew then that she was ours. Learning her name solidified it. Seeing her picture confirmed it. And when we met her, that was it: we were hers. No maybes, what ifs, doubts. That was it, unconditionally.

Christina Perri (I know it is like pulling out a ripe Stilton to quote a song, but I feel she sums it up perfectly) says in her song 'thousand years' ; 'But watching you stand alone? All of my doubt suddenly goes away somehow, one step closer. I have died every day waiting for you, darling don't be afraid for I will love you for a thousand years, I'll love you for a thousand more...'

It is a strange oddity going through the adoption process, especially FFA because you live with a sense of uncertainty on a daily basis, but when that uncertainty starts to fade away you are left with relief and gratitude that you have been chosen to be bigs to a teeny wee human.

On the 20th December we will be legally the parents we have been for nearly six months, and we will never be able to articulate the gratitude for having been chosen to be our teeny wee human's bigs.

Chapter 13
Disorgansied chaos: waiting for dates

The one thing that you become well versed with when you start the adoption process is that you will soon become adept at living in a sea of disorganised chaos, which is ironic really because when you become a big to a teeny wee human you have to become supremely organised otherwise you will never leave the house... or it will take you days to 'nip to the shops' rather than the minutes it used to in 'life pre-teeny wee human'.

The further through the journey you travel, you would expect that you would become the master winging it, as your cape is securely fastened to the seat of your pants, but alas, the further down the path you go the more frustrating you find the disorganised chaos. It is frustrating because the disorganisation usually comes from the policy makers and institutions that are holding you to emotional ransom for 'however long it takes' to get your permanence: your forever.

You have put in an Olympic heptathlete performance, Fosbury flopped every hurdle you have been faced with, applied for court and now you wait for your court date to be announced. Now, anyone who knows me knows that I am not patient at the best of times, and stupid just irritates me. Dealing with court was no exception. We submitted the paperwork (recorded super special delivery and everything), tracked the delivery, phoned the court to pay our fees within 24-hours, and then were told the paperwork was with the judge. It seemed to be with the judge for ages: either because they were slow at reading or because they had a large pile of other bits of paper to read through…or so we thought. In your paperwork you write down the contact at the adoption agency for the court to contact if they require any further information: this should be straight forward, you'd think! The court required more information from the agency, but rather than contacting the appropriate social worker, they emailed someone who was on leave, so it sat in an inbox, somewhere at the council offices, unanswered, until I started to ask specific questions of the court and could solve the issue that the court had created by not reading their own forms. We had now waited a couple of weeks…waiting! (The skill we can now add onto our CVs as being experts in). Once the fart in the lift had dissipated, we received the court date for the 'directions hearing' and an indication of when the 'final hearing' would be heard.

Again, irony is not the escapologist it professes to be - we informed the social workers of the court hearing dates and times. You would think that it would be court and social services who would be more organised than the bedraggled, exhausted and malfunctioning typewriter Bigs.

Chapter 14
The judgement

'They may not have my eyes, they may not have my smile, but they have all my heart.' – Unknown

Our court hearing started at 10am on the 20th December 2018. We were not allowed to attend as the birth humans are invited, so we had to go about our day as 'normal'. And like any 'normal' day in the life of a big, by 10am I had showered and dressed myself and the teeny wee human. I had put in a load of washing, hung it out and put in another load. Tidied the house, hoovered the carpets, swept and mopped the floors, all whilst entertaining a teeny wee human and messaging my fellow Big who was being 'normal' at work.

I worked on the premise – and because the paperwork said so – that the court hearing would last 30 minutes (and as it is court, they wouldn't go on for longer). 10.30am came and went, as did 10.45am and 11am was just around the corner – I felt sick, my fellow Big felt distracted and we were both holding our breaths and phones waiting for Mavis to phone us with news. At 10.55am my phone rang and Mavis told me that the Judge had ruled and we were now parents – officially and legally – to our teeny wee human.

Now this, this was the moment, the moment that you can finally exhale, completely, without reservation, out until the whole of your body relaxes and gives into the emotion you have contained in your body for the last 800 days. I cried. And I got to call my fellow Big to tell him that finally we were mum and dad: legally, forever!

No more pee needed

Yesterday we had our final pee on stick, holy crap bags, these are happy tears, moment. Yesterday we heard those words you feel you wait a lifetime to hear 'it's official, you are mum and dad!'

I have mentioned before that adoption is a series of pee on stick moments. Moments that give you a blast of hurrah, followed by a moment of oh lord this has just got real, but in spite of how many steps you take forward you always feel as though the' forever' will never come and that the 'happily ever after' is a thing of legends or stories spun to give hope to the feeble minded. Well, stuff that for a game of soldiers (yes, I have just used a dad phrase)… Forever does exist and it is real, a little like fairies and unicorns: it is if you believe it is.

The beautiful thing about our 'journey' (because that is what we call experiences lol) is that we have never been short of support and kindness from people, and the most amazing thing is that it has often come from the most unlikely of places. Adoption, and I guess being a first time big, can make you feel like you are stranded on an island with one faulty armband, a spoon with holes in, and a Blue Peter mock up of Tracy Island: clueless and armed with a load of useless crap that you just need to make work. But not once have I felt, in all my woeful incompetence, judged negatively for being clueless, finding it hard or for flapping like a penguin trying to take off.

What I am trying to articulate in my roundabout way is that we, my fellow big, teeny wee human, and I, are now officially a family: forever. And all of our supportive humans have been part of our journey and should raise a glass because you have been part of something a little bit lovely.

And, no more pee is needed… Until next time… Maybe.

Chapter 15
There is always one more hurdle to get through: waiting for appeal

You are mum and dad, legally and forever, but… the birth humans have 21 days to appeal. That is 21 days that you do not worry about or fixate on. They are days that your family worries about because they have danced on the periphery of your journey for the duration because adoption is your path and your family can only stand, watch and wait for you to get your happily ever after. They worry with you and for you and knowing that you still have 21 days to wait for the smallest and tiniest risk of the birth humans appealing is a burden they carry for you.

You don't want the birth humans to appeal: your teeny wee human is your child and is forever! But it makes your heart a little sad that they did not fight, not even a little bit, for the wee human you have fought for since before you knew them.

Chapter 16
Celebration

It takes a village. It really does! The journey through adoption is a series of moments that should be celebrated and marked because you overcome so much to get your forever. We have been so lucky to have a village of people across the globe who have cheered for us throughout our adoption journey. When you finally get to the end, you get to celebrate, and that celebration starts with the court putting the final full stop to your process and marking the first day as a forever family.

Your celebration hearing is a moment. You go to court, for the first and last time in your adoption, and sit, surrounded by your family and social workers, in front of a judge who drops the gavel for the last time. It is a wonderful and emotional moment that you won't ever forget.

There is not much left to say on your celebration really, except that in spite of all the frustrations and hurdles you face throughout the adoption process, celebrate the moments because there are many.

What's in a name???

This week was yet another big week for my fellow big and I... And the teeny wee human. This week we heard the final drop of the gavel in court and our teeny wee human's name be declared. It is funny because for so long you consider the name, you have to say it, write it, and read it... But until that gavel drops it doesn't belong to you. Until that moment, when your family is formed through adoption, they carry your name in heart and spirit but not legally.

Not only did we get the final sign, sealed and delivered moment, we also had our teeny wee human's naming ceremony and celebration. And for me, the beautiful thing was that so many people who had supported us from the wings were there to join us in that moment, and of those people there were those we now call friends who have travelled our path through adoption but are walking their own journey.

We were lucky to have our local inter-faith council agree to do our teeny wee human's naming ceremony, and to accept her into the faiths they represent, and bless her in the name of all. We thought long and hard about how we wanted the ceremony to be as neither my fellow big and I follow a specific religion, we just try to live by the values they all teach: be kind, help others, do no harm… So we had the ceremony outside amongst nature. It was perfect.

Shakespeare said 'what's in a name? It is nor hand, nor foot, nor arm, nor face, nor any other part belonging to a man.' I shall tell you what a name is… A name does not define who you are or what you shall become, it is something that shows you are part of something, you are wanted and you belong… Because that is just it, our teeny wee human is part of us and our family, she was wanted from the day we heard about her, and she belongs to us (not in a possessive way olde world, days gone by way) as we belong to her because, in the words of Sister Sledge 'we are family'.

Chapter 17
And that's a wrap

So, after 800 ish days (officially) and 9 ½ years our adoption journey is complete. I have learnt a lot during our ***Babytism of Fire*** and still accept that I am 99% clueless and a true example of a paint-by-numbers mum. We may have been dropped into the eye of the storm when our teeny wee human parachuted her way into our life, but we held on and navigated our way to forever together.

> The Alchemist says *'I love you because the entire universe conspired to help me find you.'*

Adoption is hard. It is frustrating and heartbreaking at times. It makes you feel powerless and vulnerable. But, it makes you resilient. It teaches you compassion, understanding and empathy in a way you didn't know exists. It fills your world with happiness and joy. Adoption, in spite of all the moments of darkness, brings you light. It is worth it. Adoption finds the heart you are meant to protect.

Ladies and gentlehumans, that I believe, is it….for now!

And so, a new chapter begins…

This week marked the start of a new chapter in the Babytism. This week was the week that the teeny wee human sprouted her teeny tiny birdy wings and took a step closer to becoming her inner Chandler Bing aka 'a strong independent woman' (or if you feel the need to be more baby-feminist, she took her first teeny weeny step towards getting in touch with her inner Beyonce).

Making the decision to take your teeny wee human to nursery is an odd thing. It is odd because you are making a deliberate decision to allow another human being the privilege of looking after your teeny wee human between the hours of 8am – 4pm (at the moment) so you can go off into the world, regain your grown-up working identity and be without the teeny wee human who has formed your entire world for the last 8 months of your life. You choose to do this for selfishly altruistic reasons.

The selfish reasons can fall into the following categories: -

- I won't have to change 100 nappies and experience the disgusting yet impressive poop capturing recepticle moments
- I will be able to have an adult conversation that does not revolve around a teeny wee person, remembering that I am a real person and I do exist in my own right.
- I like money: Statutory Adoption Pay (SAP) or Statutory Maternity Pay (SMP) is crap, you couldn't live off it for long, and when that money well dries up, it is fresh air and leftovers that will sustain your life.

The beautifully altruistic reasons for placing the teeny wee human into nursery outweigh the selfish ones 10-fold: -

- It is so good for the teeny wee human to be around other teeny wee humans so that she learns how to play, take turns, socialise, and accept different people into her teeny wee world.

- It makes her teeny wee world safely bigger than me and my fellow big, whilst still making me and my fellow big the centre of her teeny wee world.
- It helps the teeny wee human to develop more: she has come on in leaps and bounds already and it has only been 5 days! She is cruising the furniture like a pro!!!
- The teeny wee human starts her education positively, so hopefully, by the time pre-school starts she will feel secure in herself so that she will be able to embrace her learning when it becomes more formal.
- The teeny wee human will develop her resilience further: learning to self-soothe is so important for teeny wee humans whilst they are growing up.

I was expecting, when I dropped the teeny wee human off at nursery for the week, that I would be faced with tears, tantrums, tiaras and snot-bubbles to end all snot-bubbles because it would mean that the teeny wee human loved me more than anyone else in the whole wide world. In reality, I did not get any of those emotive moments. And, even though I felt emotional in my squishy insides, I did not boo hoo when I dropped her off at nursery either. Now, that doesn't mean that I don't care that I am leaving my teeny wee human in nursery, it means the absolute opposite…but, we are lucky enough to have found a nursery who we trust and who has taken on board every single thing that we have told them about our teeny wee human so I have not felt concerned that they will not look after our teeny wee human. Our teeny wee human may not have belted out a complete Alison Moyet version of 'All cried out' when I leave, which is because she knows she is safe, she is a happy little sausage, and I am there, without fail, at the end of the day – early even – to pick her up. When I do come and collect her, the moment I walk through the door she smiles, squeals with happiness and reaches for me! It is the highlight of my day! AND when my fellow big joins with me on the nursery collection run, we get a doubley squeally squeal and bounces of joy, lots of reaching for cuddles and a very happy little face.

The Babytism of Fire

But nursery does not start at nursery, no! It starts at the moment your eyes slowly force their way open at 6am before the teeny wee human wakes, as you have a set amount of time to get yourself showered before the impending juggling act commences.

So you thought you could multi-task when your teeny wee human was home full-time with you………………how wrong you are! How wrong I was!!! I thought the morning juggle would be a doddle, because I can brush my teeth, prepare a bottle, hold a baby, whilst answering the door, sending a text, making an appointment and ironing, all without dropping the baby, getting toothpaste on my top or burning a hole in a single item of clothing. Now, when being 'work ready' gets into the occasion, you have to be more cautious as you don't want to cause an outfit change (yours) because of puke or leaky poop getting on your clothes and a) you notice, and b) you don't notice and end up walking around work all-day with the smell of poop and puke following you around like a small yappy dog – annoying and won't go away!

Five days in, and our routine has gone from cuddly and slow, to less cuddly until everyone is ready and efficient.

Eyes snap (who am I kidding) slowly force their way open at 6am, I roll out of bed whilst reinstating my spectacles to my face so I can see where I am going…start the 'Oh my god!' mental statement, followed by 'how it is still dark, I am sure we are now in summer time', and '6am!!!!! it feels like the middle of the night. Kill me! Kill me now!' as I stumble down the old apples and pears. Enter the kitchen, make medicine for the teeny wee human, pop it in the fridge. Light on in the bathroom – retinas feel like they are burning as the lights are like the sun – shower on, shower, get out. Upstairs. Fellow big gets the teeny wee human from her pit of slumber, whilst I start to get dressed. Tag team: fellow big shower and coffee, me teeny wee human duty whilst trying to make my face more socially acceptable whilst spotting the teeny human who has the need to embrace being adventurous and attempt to crawl off the bed. Pause making my face socially acceptable until fellow big and coffee return up the apples and pears with medicine too. The rest is a mash-up of who is getting ready, who is keeping a watchful eye on the teeny wee human, making breakfast, eating it (us….the teeny wee human has to wait until she has been medicated for 30 minutes). I get to about 80% ready when my fellow big makes the teeny wee humans breakfast and I feed her, as he bids his fond farewells to go to work. The remaining 15 minutes before leaving the house is usually one of carnage, panic and poop! maybe an outfit change – hers not mine. But, not once have we been late! And…I have only gone to work with puke on me once. I would say that is a victory! and a big hooray for teamwork!

(I am dreading the day that my fellow big has to go to work before 6am and I have to Hans Solo (I am assuming he is some sort of lone space man until he finds Luke Skywalker and Princess Leia, hence the name) my way through the morning routine.)

Printed in Poland
by Amazon Fulfillment
Poland Sp. z o.o., Wrocław